VICTORY IN THE MIDST OF ADVERSITY

Moving forward in difficult times

CARLTON E. HADLEY, JR

Copyright ©2014 Carlton E. Hadley, Jr. All rights reserved

Victory In The Midst Of Adversity

Moving forward in difficult times

By Carlton E. Hadley, Jr.

All rights reserved. The author guarantees all contents are original and do not infringe upon the legal rights of any other person or work. No part of this book shall be reproduced, stored or transmitted by any means without the sole, written consent of the author.

Unless otherwise noted, Scripture taken from the New King James Version.

Copyright © 1982 by Thomas Nelson, Inc.

Used by permission. All rights reserved.

ISBN -13:978-0692303900

The Kingdom's Scribe Publishing

Atlanta, Georgia

Printed in the United States of America

Dedication

To My Parents:

Carlton E. Hadley, Sr.

&

The late Ruby L. Hadley (1944-2012)

Though we were not the Huxtables (The Cosby Show), you two have managed to raise one who will speak to nations through the gift of writing. Thank you for all of your support and faith in me even at times when I had no faith in myself. I love you both very much.

I would first like to give glory and honor to God for making this endeavor possible.

Proverbs 18:16, *"A man's gift makes room for him and brings him before great men."*

Special thanks to: My wife 4 life and grace gift, *La'Shaun Hadley*. You've endured the highs, lows and all of the circumstances of life that has brought this book to light. Hang in there Baby, our plans will work this time. This is our catch up year!!

My beautiful children, *Shy'Nada, Carlton III and Quinton*. You three are definitely living testimonies as to how to "keep it moving." Despite all of the negative conditions you all have experienced, you three continue to strive for excellence. Thanks for believing in me. I am proud of you all.

My Spiritual Coverings: *Apostle Derrick and Pastor Charmaine Flanagan, Sr.* Apostle thank you for fathering me in this gospel ministry. In spite of my faults, bad decisions and seasons of disobedience, you never saw me as less than a Man of God.

To *Linda Boykin*: Thanks for your keen eye, professional editing and for staying on top of me to make sure this project was completed. Love you!

To *Louise Shepherd-Savage*: With all of the troubles and trials that you did see overtake me and almost ruin my destiny, not once did you abandon me or fail to impart an encouraging word into me. How can that debt ever be repaid?

Thanks to every member of my family, that is both natural and spiritual. To those who inspired me and to those who doubted me, I really am grateful. To those who thought I was not qualified and to those who always knew that greatness resided within me, thank you. To all of the great men and women of God who has spoken into and over my life, especially those of the 7000 More Covenant Fellowship (Continual Blessings Apostle H.L. "Skip" and Pastor Alicia Horton)

To those that I did not thank by mentioning your name in this book, do not think that your contribution in my life is minimal or not appreciated. Thank you for every prayer, every kind gesture, every word of encouragement and every gift of love.

I love you all!

Always writing to inspire and encourage,
Carlton E. Hadley, Jr.
The Kingdom's Scribe

Contents

Preface	1
Introduction	2
Chapter 1. The Plan of Victory	5
A Prayer for Courage	16
Chapter 2. Victorious Because of a Vision	17
A Prayer for Vision	24
Chapter 3. The Voice of Victory	25
A War Cry Prayer	32
Chapter 4. The Weapons of Warfare	33
A Warfare Prayer	40
Chapter 5. No Retreat	41
A Prayer for Victory	49

Preface

There is an old spiritual (gospel song) that I remember hearing my mother listen to when I was a child. I don't know the title of the song nor can I recall the artist who sings it, but the lead singer would say something to the likes of "if you've never had any rain to fall in your life, just wait awhile." That rain that the singer was referring to was trouble or adversity. And just as sure as the day turns to night and the sun gives way to the moon, at some juncture(s) in your life you will experience some difficult times. Jesus even declared in John 16:33 that *"in this world you will have tribulation."* Just because we experience trouble or hard times in our lives, it doesn't mean that we accept those moments as a way of life. It is my prayer dear friend, that as you read this book, the keys and strategies for living a victorious life and moving forward in triumph are revealed to you by the Spirit of God. May you gain the wisdom, courage, and faith needed to defeat your adversary and overcome every obstacle that may be placed in your way many times over.

Introduction

For many believers, the thought of achieving victory conjures up pleasant images of every area of our lives in perfect harmony with nothing missing and nothing broken. Though this is a very popular belief as it pertains to the blessings of God, for a great many of us, circumstances and situations in our lives are very much out of tune, out of alignment, out of whack, and adversity seems to challenge us at every turn. As the Apostle Paul states in II Corinthians 4:8-9, ***(8) "We are hard-pressed on every side, yet not crushed; we are perplexed but not in despair; (9) persecuted, but not forsaken; struck down, but not destroyed."*** This should be encouragement for the sons of God that despite some unfavorable and even some uncomfortable conditions in our lives, victory is available to the believer. Victory is our portion and our inheritance according to I John 5:4 ***"For whatsoever is born of God overcomes the world. And this is the victory that has overcome the world-our faith."*** Armed with this knowledge, we as believers must stand in our place of victory and not be moved by the situations that come to persuade us to forfeit the triumph that Jesus Christ has already gained and provided for us. Most of the saints that we read about in the scriptures faced great opposition and adversity in their walk with God, yet overcoming limitations and being the victor was the ultimate goal in every endeavor. Hard times, as difficult as this may be to receive, are designed to foster your trust in God more so than when things are going well for you. You are more inclined to seek assistance outside of the realm of humanity when your back is against the wall and your options are limited or when no other options are presented except to stand and fight. Let us consider David in I Samuel 30:1-6. *(1) "Now* it happened, when David and his men came to Ziklag, on the third day, that the Amalekites had invaded the South and Ziklag, attacked Ziklag and burned it with fire, (2) And had taken captive the women and those who were there, from small to great; and they did not kill anyone but carried them away. (3) So David and his men came to the city, and there it was, burned with fire; and their wives, their sons, and their daughters had been taken captive. (4) Then David and the people who were with him lifted up their voices and wept, until they had no more power to weep. (5) And David's two wives, Ahinoam the Jezreelitess, and Abigail the widow of Nabal the Carmelite, had been taken captive. (6) Now David was greatly distressed, for the people spoke of stoning him, because the soul of all the people was grieved, every man for his sons and his daughters. But David strengthened himself in the Lord his God." Can you imagine the shock that David and his soldiers experienced as they saw smoke billowing in the air from a distance while approaching their city? These men were walking into a literal hell on earth. Their village had been plundered, burned to the ground, and all of the women and children were taken as prisoners of war. Certainly this was devastating even for these battle-hardened men of war, for the scripture states that these men wept until they could weep no more. Can you fathom the anguish and the fear that gripped their hearts by not knowing if their children or their spouses were still alive? The fear and grief that engrossed these soldiers soon gave way to fury as talk arose of stoning their leader, King David. Although the anger of his followers were aroused against him and even in the midst of his own grief and distress, David encouraged himself in the Lord according to verse six. When it seemed like all was lost, David turned to the God who had proven himself to be a victorious deliverer on numerous occasions. How could he forget about being empowered to slay a lion and a bear while tending to his father's sheep? And surely he remembered the victory against a menacing, God-forsaking giant with no armor or sword, but being armed with only a sling and five smooth stones. What would make this situation any different than the other difficult places that David had found himself in before? I can only imagine him saying in his heart, **"if God be for me, who can be against me?"** (Romans 8:31). Many of you reading this book may be at your own personal Ziklag where everything has gone up in smoke. You may have lost some things and even some people may have left your life and now you feel empty and depleted, like all of your fight and zeal is gone. Some of you may be asking, Lord why ME!!? Why do I have to experience this or your question may be where do I go from here? Better yet, you may be in a dry season where nothing is growing and prosperity seems to evade you. Do not be discouraged my friend, **"for there is the sound of an abundance of rain."**(I Kings 18:41). Even at your place of Ziklag, God has eternally secured your victory through our Lord and Savior Jesus Christ. So my brother and my sister trust in the Lord with all your heart so that he may produce a great victory in your life.

CHAPTER 1

THE PLAN OF VICTORY

Imagine for a moment if you would, that every time you squared off against an opponent you were assured beforehand that you could not and would not lose. The only stipulation is that you had to follow the fight strategy or game plan to the letter. It doesn't matter how mighty or fierce your opponent may be, you will win. Most of us would undoubtedly face our competition with an air of confidence and probably a slight touch of arrogance because we know that we are going to be declared the winner. According to the Holy Scriptures, we have that kind of assurance of total victory for our lives which is found in II Corinthians 2:14a, **"Now thanks be unto God who always causes us to triumph in Christ Jesus."** The word always implies that "at all times" we are triumphant or victorious even when life's situations try to dictate otherwise. The Lord God clearly demonstrates to us through the scriptures that as long as we remain in him, we remain on the winning side. I John 3:8b proclaims, ***"For this purpose was the Son of God manifested, that He may destroy the works of the devil."*** Jesus came to disarm our adversary so that we may have perpetual victory. Since the subject of this book is victory in adverse circumstances, let us take a look and see how victory is defined. **Victory is the overcoming of an enemy or antagonist; achievement of mastery or success in a struggle or endeavor against odds or difficulties.** Simply put, victory is the act of conquering or defeating any opposition that stands in your way. All throughout the scriptures God lays out his elaborate plan of total victory for our lives. ***"Plans of peace and not evil, to give you a future, a hope, and to bring you to an expected end."*** (Jeremiah 29:11)

STICK WITH THE PLAN

When we commit ourselves to become students of the Bible, we will soon discover that our Jehovah God is a man of war. A God who despises evil, ***"teaching my hands to make war, so that my arms can bend a bow of bronze."*** (II Samuel 22:35).

No great leader would send his troops into a firefight without a detailed plan of attack. Included in that plan is a strategy for victory. No man enters a war or competition with an expectation of defeat. Time and again we as believers can't advance against our adversary because of our defeatists' attitude. We fail to study our battle plan and often times we do not fully obey God, hence giving the devil opportunity to literally wear us out. It is often said that if you fail to plan, you plan to fail. That same adage can be applied to our spiritual lives. Numerous times we suffer loss and defeat simply because we fail to study (and follow) the plan of God for our lives which is the word of God. It has to be more than once or twice a week because we are engaged in a spiritual battle every single day of our lives. At other times we may study and even hear the voice of God yet still fail to properly execute those things that we've been instructed to do. Isaiah 1:19-20 declares that, **(19) "If you be willing and obedient, you shall eat the good of the land; (20) But if you refuse and rebel, you shall be devoured by the sword."** Many of us (myself included) miss it right there because of that small word called obedience. We fail to **fully** execute the plan of God often succumbing to the mind of reasoning and trying to make sense out of what the Lord has said. One thing that I have learned during my faith journey is that when you are going through difficult times or as my Apostle calls it, "in between blessings," is that God will release a word of faith into your life and it will leave you stunned and speechless because in your spirit you do receive it, however in the natural realm, that is your flesh, you say how can this thing be. It is during those moments that we must be able to recognize the sure voice of God and completely obey his commands so that his supernatural resources will yield itself unto us. What if Elijah had refused to follow the plan or instructions that God had laid out for him in I Kings 17:1-16, **(1) "And Elijah the Tishbite, of the inhabitants of Gilead, said to Ahab, As the Lord God of Israel lives, before whom I stand, there shall not be dew or rain these years, except at my word."(2) Then the word of the Lord came to him, saying, (3) Get away from here and turn eastward, and hide by the Brook Cherith, which flows into the Jordan. (4) And it will be that you shall drink from the brook, and I have commanded the ravens to feed you there. (5) So he went and did according to the word of the Lord, for he went and stayed by the Brook Cherith which** *flows into the Jordan. (6) The ravens brought him bread and meat in the morning, and bread and meat in the evening; and he drank from the brook. (7) And it happened after a while that the brook dried up, because there had been no rain in the land. (8) Then the word of the Lord came to him, saying, (9) Arise, go to Zarephath, which belongs to Sidon, and dwell there. See, I have commanded a widow woman there to provide for you. (10) So he arose and went to Zarephath. And when he came to the gate of the city, indeed a widow was there gathering sticks. And he called to her and said, Please bring me a little water in a cup that I may drink. (11) And as she was going to get it, he called to her and said, Please bring me a morsel of bread in your hand. (12) So she said, As the Lord our God lives, I do not have bread, only a handful of flour in a bin, and a little oil in a jar; and see I am gathering a couple of sticks that I may go in and prepare it for myself and my son, that we may eat it and die. (13) and Elijah said to her, Do not fear; go and do as you have said, but make me a small cake from it first, and bring it to me; and afterward make some for you and your son. (14) For thus says the Lord of Israel; The bin of flour shall not be used up, nor shall the jar of oil run dry, until the day the Lord sends rain on the earth. (15) So she went away and did according to the word of Elijah; and she and he and her household ate for many days. (16) The bin of flour was not used up, nor did the jar of oil run dry, according to the word of the Lord which He spoke by Elijah."* After Elijah had declared a drought in the land because of the idolatrous worship of King Ahab, God gave him clear instructions to hide by the Brook Cherith. Bread and meat, both in the morning and the evening with special delivery by ravens. Herein is a miracle in and of itself for ravens by nature are scavengers, so they could have easily devoured the meat that was intended for the prophet. However what happens in verse 7 through 16 is more than miraculous. It is astonishing and should provide motivation for us to obey the will of God for our lives. Here in this passage both of these individuals are in a hard place. The brook had dried up and the supernatural food deliveries had ceased for the man of God and here was the widow woman who was down to her very last, with no hope for another day. I can only imagine if you would allow that the man of God had to contemplate a few things in his mind. At the place I was beforehand, the water and food disappeared and now you've sent me to Zarephath to be sustained by a widow woman who doesn't have enough for those who are already apart of her household. Have you ever been there before? God has told you to move and has given you a word that he is with you and will sustain you at that place, yet when you start to move it seems as if where he has sent you is worse than the place he brought you from. Notice I used the word "seems," because often what we see or perceive in the natural realm is actually something far greater than what we can imagine in the spiritual realm. This is the place where God is developing your eyes of faith so that you can then begin to walk by faith and not by sight. God has to get us to that place where we no longer rely on our intellect or ability to analyze thus drawing our own conclusions about the situation. God sends us to our Zarephaths so that our trust in him can be fully tested. Zarephath is a place where we acquire a nevertheless mentality when we can then proclaim that, **"God is not a man that he should lie, Nor a son of man that he should repent. Has He said, and will he not do? Or has He spoken, and will He not make it good?** (Numbers 23:19)

Elijah could not be moved by what he beheld with his natural eyes, but he had to hold fast to the word of the Lord. Sometimes we also find ourselves in these do or die situations and the Lord is constantly challenging us to follow his plan and to do all of his will. You may be at your very own Brook Cherith and God is leading you to Zarephath or you may even be in the brickyard of Pharaoh and awaiting deliverance from the bondage that is currently plaguing your life. No matter where you are, God has a plan of victory for your life that causes the heavens to open up and yield its supernatural resources unto you. Be encouraged my friend, it's not over until God says it's over. Stick with the plan and obey God fully.

COURAGE IS A MUST

Sticking with the plan of God in order to obtain victory in your life can appear at times to be a daunting task. When the cares of this life and various circumstances arise that attempt to set you back, it's easy to just cave in and give up. Mind you, I said giving up and quitting is easy. To keep forging ahead when the odds are clearly stacked against you requires an element of faith called courage. **Courage is defined as the quality of being brave: the ability to face danger, difficulty, uncertainty and pain without being overcome by fear or being deflected from a chosen course of action.** In other words, your tribulation won't cause you to change your favorable opinion about God. During moments of great stress or duress, these are often the times when the believer tends to let go of God instead of letting go of their worries and allowing God to work in their lives. I'll say amen to that from personal experience! It is in these intense moments of warfare, deep in the trenches, that we will receive our greatest deliverance if we don't give up. God is ready to do a new thing in you, through you and for you, just be strong and full of courage. If the Lord has made you a promise or has allowed his spokesmen in the earth to speak a word of prophecy concerning you, it will require you to have an unflinching amount of courage to see that promise come to pass. Let's examine the word that the Lord spoke to Joshua. *(3) "Every place that the sole of your foot will tread upon I have given you, as I said to Moses. (4) From the wilderness and this Lebanon as far as the great river, the River Euphrates, all the land of the Hittites, and to the Great Sea toward the going down of the sun, shall be your territory. (5) No man shall be able to stand before you all the days of your life; as I was with Moses, so I will be with you. I will not leave you nor forsake you. (6) Be strong and of good courage, for to this people you shall divide as an inheritance the land which I swore unto their fathers to give them. (7) Only be strong and very courageous, that you may observe to do according to all the law which Moses My servant commanded you; do not turn from it to the right hand or to the left, that you may prosper wherever you go. (8) This book of the Law shall not depart from your mouth, but you shall meditate in it day and night, that you may observe to do according to all that is written in it. For then you will make your way prosperous, and then you will have good success. (9) Have I not commanded you to be strong and of good courage; do not be afraid, nor dismayed, for the Lord your God is with you wherever you go."* (Joshua 1:3-9) Yes indeed the land of Canaan was promised to the Israelites but they had to dispossess the current inhabitants of the land. Even for us there are some things that God has promised us and we are going to have to dispossess the current possessors of our stuff. It's going to take a holy violence to reclaim and recover all of our promised possessions, whether they are of a spiritual or material nature. The Kingdom of God is certainly in need of courageous soldiers, warriors if you will, who won't buckle every time Satan shows up to persuade you to doubt the word of the Lord. Courage is a character trait that allows you to keep fighting and to keep pressing although the conditions don't seem to be in your favor. Courage says that regardless of what obstacles or opposition you may face, I will not abandon the work God has called me to. Still courage is a quality that cannot be taught but it comes from within you. It is a deep resolve within your spirit that drives out fear and replaces it with confidence and faith. II Sam 23:11-12 gives an amazing account of courage in an individual named Shammah. **(11) "And after him was Shammah the son of Agee the Hararite. The Philistines had gathered together into a troop where there was a piece of ground full of lentils. So the people fled from the Philistines. (12) But he stationed himself in the middle of the field, defended it, and killed the Philistines. So the Lord brought about a great victory."** That's true courage when you are willing to stand and fight even when everyone else around you has abandoned the ship. What do you do when you are by yourself? Do you have enough fortitude to continue in warfare or is your spiritual progress stunted because no one else is doing what you do? If the truth be told, for a great portion of the body of Christ, our flesh is what keeps us from experiencing the total victory that God desires for us to walk in. Courage is needed in order to protect the anointing of God in your life. It's a simple task to become what others and even what your adversary says about you or to succumb to always settling for the less and accepting everything that life throws your way. That's not the way it is supposed to be. I believe in my spirit that often God is waiting on us to pursue the promises, but we lose heart and become fearful because of the obstacles and barriers that are placed in our paths. We then place limits on God and even ourselves because we lack the capacity to believe that the Lord is able to deliver us from every affliction. Take for instance the 12 spies that Moses had sent out to scout the Promised Land. Even after they saw with their very own eyes the land and the fruit that God had sworn to give them, 10 of the spies gave a negative or evil report to Moses because of fear and lack of confidence in the promise that God had made. They were cowards and could not believe what God had vowed because of the great opposition *(giants in the land)* that they faced. They were literally moved or discouraged by what they saw. Here the Lord was trying to get them to an abundant and rich land, a land where they could plant and then harvest what had been planted. Needless to say, their limited way of thinking would not even allow them to partake of it. Numbers 13:26-33 gives this account. **"(26) Now they departed and came back to Moses and Aaron and all the congregation of the children of Israel in the Wilderness of Paran, at Kadesh; they brought back word to them and to all the congregation, and showed them the fruit of the land. (27) Then they told him, and said: We went to the land where you sent us. It truly flows with milk and honey, and this is its fruit. (28) Nevertheless the people who dwell in the land are strong; the cities are fortified and very large; moreover we saw the descendants of Anak there. (29) The Amalekites dwell in the land of the South; the Hittites, the Jebusites, and the Amorites dwell in the mountains; and the Canaanites dwell by the sea and the banks of the Jordan. (30) Then Caleb quieted the people before Moses, and said, Let us go up at once and take possession, for we are well able to overcome it. (31)**

But the men who had gone up with him said, We are not able to go up against the people, for they are stronger than we. (32) And they gave the children of Israel an evil report of the land which they had spied out, saying, The land through which we have gone as spies is a land that devours its inhabitants, and all the people whom we saw in it are men of great stature. (33) There we saw the giants (The descendants of Anak came from the giants); and we were like grasshoppers in our own sight, and so we were in their sight." People of God you've got to be able to see yourself being or in the act of becoming victorious. The number one step in becoming is that you first must be able to see it. If you can see it, you can become it. The question to you now is how do you see? What do you see? Do you see yourself overcoming low self-esteem and depression? Have you been able to envision your life being free from the grips of poverty and lack? Can you see yourself totally delivered and totally set free? Are you able to visualize yourself in right standing with God? Stop being paralyzed with fear because you face a little opposition. Anytime you purpose in your heart to do all of the will of God, opposition and adversity will come. However, this is not the time to give up or quit, but that is the time to take a stand and to believe that your God is well able to cause you to triumph over your adversary and bring you to a place of complete deliverance and victory. The United States Marines use a common saying amongst the soldiers called "adapt and overcome." This is more than just a nice catch phrase. It's an attitude that says just because the conditions change, the mission remains the same. A person with this frame of mind looks for every way to remove or eliminate hindrances and barriers. Now is the time for the children of God to adapt and overcome where we will begin to view our opposition as an opportunity for God to show himself strong. Then we can begin to see our set-backs as a set up for a great comeback. At this moment, your world may not look like your potential, but you must keep pressing into God until the manifestation of your promise appears. Strengthen and encourage yourself in the Lord your God and continually envision yourself as the victor and not the victim. See yourself full of God's power. Carry yourself as a mighty conqueror and let us banish the grasshopper mentality to outer darkness. Lastly my friend, endeavor to accomplish all of the will of God that he has for your life even in the midst of your difficult times. Tough circumstances tend to produce tough survivors. Only be though strong and very courageous.

A PRAYER FOR COURAGE

Dear Lord,

Thank you in advance for imparting the spirit of courage into those who are reading this book. Allow their faith to be increased and their hearts to be strengthened so that they won't give up and will continue to fight until the manifestation of your promises appears in their lives. Give them the strength to stick with the plan that you have prepared for them, for they shall work this time. Releasing these words of faith in Jesus' name,

Amen.

CHAPTER 2

VICTORIOUS BECAUSE OF A VISION

One of the key components of living a victorious life is that you must be able to see or visualize yourself living victoriously. In other words, you must have a vision for your victory. Now we are not talking about vision from a theological perspective, but vision from a ***"faith-o-logical"*** context where you believe what God has said despite the adverse consequences that you may be presently experiencing. Vision in laymen's terms is simply the ability to see what God is saying. To see biblically speaking, means to understand and when you understand what God has purposed for your life, you won't allow life's challenges or hard times to deter you from pursuing victory. In order for us to become the ***"head and not the tail, above only and not beneath, the lender and not the borrower,"*** (Deuteronomy 28:13) we must have vision.

Victory is the vision that God has placed before every believer. I John 5:4-5 explains it in this manner. ***"(4) For whatever is born of God overcomes the world. And this is the victory that has overcome the world-our faith. (5) Who is he that overcomes the world, but he who believes that Jesus is the Son of God?"*** What a powerful assurance for those who serve the Lord. When you take an honest assessment of most of the troubles that you've encountered in your life, you'll discover that these were attempts to kill the vision that God has placed within you. Though times may be a little rough for you at the present time, the Lord desires to deliver you to a good and a large land, to a land that flows with milk and honey. Right away you must get a vision of that land and not be detoured by what's happening around you. Having vision from God is very important because it allows you to view your world differently. Natural sight says my situation is hopeless. You begin to think that things are always going to be this way or I don't see how it's going to get any better. Vision says that in spite of the fact that a dry season is upon me, ***"there is a sound of an abundance of rain"*** (I Kings 18:41). Vision declares that I'm somewhere in the future and I look much better than I look right now. Do you see what I'm saying?

THE FAITH FACTOR

I have heard vision defined as the energy behind every effort and the force that pushes through all the problems that occur. When times get hard (and at one time or another they will) vision is what helps to pull you through those weak moments. When you feel like walking away vision reminds you of what lies ahead. That is why it is so important that you get a picture of where God is taking you. This picture or vision is what will propel you and drive you to your destiny even when circumstances are not favorable in your life. It will push you through all opposition because you know that this hardship is temporary. You can stand in confidence and declare that things will change or are changing because God has given you a vision for victory. He has allowed you to conceptualize a day that you have not yet seen before. Vision is what allows us to look away from our present situation and to see what the Lord has already done. It is possible however to have obscured vision and not fully operate in the liberty that God has called us to. What do you mean by that I hear you ask? God can give us a vision for a particular area of our lives and we say receive it, yet we never pursue it because we lack faith. Faith is assurance, trust and confidence in the ability of our God. Hebrews 4:2 declares, **"For indeed the gospel was preached to us as well as them; but the word which they heard did not profit them, not being mixed with faith in those who heard it."** My prayer is that this will not be your testimony. One of the worst experiences that you can endure is to have a vision from God that does not come to fruition. Imagine the anguish and sorrow Moses must have felt as God allowed him to view the Promised Land and in the same breath declared that he would not enter in. **"(1) Then Moses went up from the plains of Moab to Mount Nebo, to the top of Pisgah, which is across from Jericho. And the Lord showed him all the land of Gilead as far as Dan, (2) all Naphtali and the land of Ephraim and Manasseh, all the land of Judah as far as the Western Sea, (3) the South, and the plain of the Valley of Jericho, the city of palm trees, as far as Zoar. (4) Then the Lord said to him, "This is the land of which I swore to give Abraham, Isaac and Jacob, saying, 'I will give it to your descendants.' I have caused you to see it with your eyes,**

but you shall not cross over there" (Deuteronomy 34:1-4). Does this passage make you squirm as you contemplate your own fate as it relates to what the Lord has shown you? And though Moses didn't get to enter into the Promised Land because of his disobedience, we also often display the same kind of disobedience by our lack of faith in what God has spoken or promised to us. Largely, having faith in God and in his ability are the missing elements in our quest to achieve a better quality of living. We tend to rely on our own ability and not on God. True or prophetic vision comes from God and you will need his supernatural help in order to see it come to pass. God's plan for your life is too grand to accomplish in your own strength. That is when faith begins to do its part. Sadly the pattern that I see in the world of Christianity is that the more we are persecuted or the more intense our afflictions are, the more we tend to lose faith. Yet it is in the furnace of our afflictions that our faith should be at its highest or strongest point. It affords us a unique opportunity to not only allow God to deliver us, but to also show unbelievers his unmatched and undeniable power. Let us examine the Hebrew boys in Daniel chapter 3:12-18. ***(12) "There are certain Jews whom you have set over the affairs of the province of Babylon: Shadrach, Meshach, and Abed-Nego; these men, O king, have not paid due regard to you. They do not serve your gods or worship the gold image which you have set up. (13) Then Nebuchadnezzar, in rage and fury, gave the command to bring Shadrach, Meshach, and Abed-Nego. So they brought these men before the king. (14) Nebuchadnezzar spoke, saying to them, is it true, Shadrach, Meshach, and Abed-Nego, that you do not serve my gods or worship the gold image that I have set up? (15) Now if you are ready at the time you hear the sound of the horn, flute, harp, lyre, and psaltery,***

in symphony with all kinds of music, and you fall down and worship the image which I have made, good! But if you do not worship, you shall be cast immediately into the midst of a burning fiery furnace. And who is the god who will deliver you from my hands? (16) Shadrach, Meshach, and Abed-Nego answered and said to the king, O Nebuchadnezzar, we have no need to answer you in this matter. (17) If that is the case, our God whom we serve is able to deliver us from the burning fiery furnace, and He will deliver us from your hand, O king. (18) But if not, let it be known to you, O king, that we do not serve your gods, nor will we worship your gold image which you have set up." What a sign of great faith! Despite being threatened with torture in a blazing fire these young men stood their ground. We will not bow down to worship your idols. Their confidence was not weakened and neither were they willing to compromise their faith in their God. If you continue to read in that same chapter, you'll discover that they were cast into the burning pit but were not consumed by the fire. The fire had no power! This is exactly what the Lord is trying to say to us in this hour. The trouble that we are currently facing has no power. We are just being stretched in the area of our faith.

THE POWER TO BELIEVE

Power is made available to you when you can believe God. Power to do what? The power to stop living beneath our means. The power to eliminate boundaries and to remove barriers from our lives. The power to break the self-imposed limitations that we have placed on ourselves because of fear and unbelief. Here is a prophetic definition of power: **The supernatural, super-abundant might and ability of God afforded to man that allows him the right and the privilege to operate in divine delegated**

authority. Power naturally defined: The ability or capacity to do something; Strength; and Control and influence. As you compare these two definitions, you can draw the conclusion that the power to believe can cause some things to happen. *"If you can believe, all things are possible to him that believes."* (Mark 9:23). If you can believe that you are victorious you shall become victorious. Nothing shall be impossible to the man that believes. If you can believe that God will increase you, you shall be increased. Your belief system is the basis upon which your victory will be obtained. To believe is to accept something as being true and real. To believe also means to think that something exists. You will never experience victory in Jesus Christ if you don't believe that this victory exists. We must be fully persuaded that what God has said about us throughout his word is true. We must begin to break the limits off of our thinking so that we can allow the blessings of the Lord to flow freely in our lives. Our capacity or ability to receive is predicated upon our ability or capacity to believe God. Jesus demonstrated this truth in Matt 13:53-58. *"(53) Now it came to pass, when Jesus had finished these parables that He departed from there. (54) When He had come to His own country, He taught them in their synagogue, so that they were astonished and said, Where did this Man get this wisdom and these mighty works? (55) Is this not the carpenter's son? Is not His mother called Mary? And His brothers James, Joses, Simon, and Judas? (56) And His sisters, are they not all with us? Where did this Man get all these things? (57) So they were offended at Him. But Jesus said to them, A prophet is not without honor except in his own country and in his own house. (58) Now He did not do many mighty works there because of their unbelief."* This is a perfect example of the power of God being restricted because of unbelief. Unbelief keeps us grounded, therefore we continue in a spiral of continued struggles, setbacks and defeat because of an inability to believe that all things are possible with God. The Lord desires that we have a definite unwavering faith so that we may have a definite experience with him. Hebrews 11:6 states it this way, *"But without faith it is impossible to please Him, for he who comes to God must believe that he is, and that He is a rewarder of those that diligently seek Him."* If you can believe it when God shows it to you in the spiritual realm then you can experience it here in the realm of the earth. When our faith is properly exercised, it allows us to see life through optimistic eyes instead of eyes of pessimism. Our problems are therefore reduced in stature because we've begun to view life through the eyes of faith. Wherever you are in life or whatever circumstances you are facing, your God, the Lord of Hosts, is able to deliver you. It is his desire to deliver but you have to participate and live a life full of faith-filled transactions. Don't be moved or shaken by your afflictions for they are designed to stretch you in your faith and bring you to a point where you place your trust fully in the Lord. Victory for you my friend is not afar off but only as close as you believe it to be. Stand firm in the faith of our God and do not be swayed by the onslaught of adverse situations and challenges that attempt to keep you focused on what you're going through instead of being focused on where God is taking you to. Remember, power is available to you when you choose to believe God. The power to believe is the power to overcome. Think B.I.G. **(Believe In God)**

A PRAYER FOR VISION

Heavenly Father,

I pray for my friends that are reading this book. I thank you for the vision that you have for his/her life. I praise you for the plans that you have already prearranged for them to achieve. I pray that they will not be discouraged by hard times, personal tragedies, and other calamities that may befall them. Father if there is one reading this book that has no vision for their life, open their eyes and reveal to them a glimpse of those things which are yet to come. I pray that their dreams will become a reality and that they will have good success in every endeavor. This I pray for my sister/brother.

In the matchless name of Jesus,

Amen.

CHAPTER 3

THE VOICE OF VICTORY

DECLARATION OF INDEPENDENCE (DOI)

During the time that I am preparing this manuscript, it is football season and here in Georgia on Friday nights football is king! From the bustling metropolitan areas to the small rural communities with a country store and one traffic light, high school stadiums are packed to crowd capacity as cross-town rivals battle for bragging rights as to who's the best in the county. Fans wake up on Saturday morning with little or no voice because they have cheered for Junior and his team for two solid hours. Why, I hear you ask? We figure that our cheers and shouts will give the players that motivating push to make a miraculous comeback from behind or to catch the game winning hail-mary pass with one second left on the clock. Now as I fast forward two days into Sunday, a lot of our churches are half-packed and the people that are there are making little to no noise at all. Do you see the disparity? The joy, excitement and cheering from Friday has subsided and gave way to dry amens or a haphazard wave of the hand if you're blessed to get that at all. Yet in the same manner that we cheered for our favorite teams on Friday night, we should be cheering an even greater cheer on Sunday for our own salvation and for the deliverance of others. In order for us to have victory over our adversary we must declare that victory by literally opening our mouths and speaking it. Declare means **to announce clearly or loudly: to state something in a plain, open or emphatic way.** In other words, to state something with great emphasis. A declaration is strong and forceful, backed by the might of the one who is declaring. Think of the United States of America's Declaration of Independence. To most of us it is nothing more than a historic artifact, but to those who drafted and created the articles, it represented an authoritative stance of liberty. In this document the founding fathers of this country were not requesting liberation from British rule; they **declared** the 13 united colonies free and clear of Great Britain's authority. Take a look at the strongly worded introduction.

"When in the course of Human events, it becomes necessary for one people to dissolve the political bands which have connected them with another, and to assume the powers of the earth, the separate and equal station to which the Laws of Nature, and of Nature's God entitles them, a decent respect to the opinion of mankind requires that they should declare the causes which impel them to the separation." Simply stated, under the sight of God we have a right to be a free people. If you were to examine the entire opening of the DOI, you will see that the original

colonists presented a strong argument for independence and even listed its faults or concerns against the British monarchy. Perhaps you still can't quite make the connection yet so I'll present it to you like this. When Satan is allowed to intimidate you constantly and to repeatedly have you in a place of frustration, victory is far from you. You relinquish or waive your rights to *"life, liberty, and the pursuit of happiness"* when you stand in the face of adversity and never declare your deliverance and liberation from demonic strongholds. Though these words are recorded in the preamble to the DOI, Jesus tells us in John 10:10 that this is the reason that he came to mankind. **"The thief does not come except to steal, and to kill, and to destroy. I have come that they may have life and have it more abundantly."** That's life…..the good life, the God life. Then II Corinthians 3:17 shows us that in God we have liberty and spiritual freedom to experience him in all of his glory. **"Now the Lord is the Spirit; and where the Spirit of the Lord is, there is liberty."** So now you see that before there was ever a DOI drafted in 1776, independence from the forces of darkness came in the person of Jesus Christ. He provided us with independence from the world system and its disorder. For we are in the world and not of it. We have independence from the spirit of inability because we **can do all things through Christ who gives us the strength.** (Philippians 4:13). We have independence from the spirit of depression because Jesus is the lifter of our heads. **"(7) Lift up your heads, O ye gates! And be ye lifted up ye everlasting doors! And the King of glory shall come in. (8) Who is this King of glory? The Lord strong and mighty, the Lord mighty in battle. Lift up you heads, O ye gates! Lift up, ye everlasting doors! And the King of glory shall come in. (10) Who is this King of glory? The Lord of hosts, He is the King of** *glory."* (Psalm 24:7-10). You must forcefully declare your victory over your circumstances and tell hell, NO! Make your decree known in the heavens and watch it become established in the earth. Declare the strength and might of the Lord in your life. Declare the glory of God in the life of your family members, co-workers, business associates and in every place that you desire to see him move. Record on paper the areas of your life in which you are declaring victory and visit it at least once a week. Constantly remind yourself and your God of what it is that you're pressing towards. Whatever you do, don't remain silent. Open your mouth, praise your God and declare your independence from anything or anyone that is preventing you from receiving God's best for your life.

THE WAR CRY

The title of this particular chapter is aptly named the voice of victory because your victory does indeed have a voice. In the previous section, we talked about declaring your victory. That's the formal, civilized way of making your intentions known. However in the heat of battle, there is a shout; a war cry that a warrior releases when he is about to engage his enemy. It is by design a loud yell or shout that encourages his fellow soldiers and simultaneously strikes fear in the heart of his enemy. I believe with all my being that God has placed a shout within all of us. To shout means to "split the ear." Though I am of a Charismatic and Pentecostal persuasion, we are not talking about dancing with fancy footwork or a two-step shuffle. But this shout that we are referring to is a fire in your belly. It is a sound of victory that is released when you open your mouth and shout. I have been trying to understand where the tradition began in Western churches of being stoic, cold and library quiet. The psalmist in Psalm 47:1 encourages us to *"shout unto God with a voice of triumph."* That means to make a high, joyful noise; an exuberant praise of jubilee! It is amazing especially for believers that we can study our bibles, see the examples that are set before us, yet we fail to embrace those practices that have proven to yield victorious results. Let us travel to Joshua 6:12-20 and see what it took to break down the walls of Jericho. ***"(12) And Joshua rose early in the morning, and the priests took up the ark of the Lord. (13) Then seven priests bearing seven trumpets of rams' horns before the ark of the Lord went on continually and blew with the trumpets. And the armed men went before them. But the rear guard came after the ark of the Lord, while the priests continued blowing the trumpets. (14) and the second day they marched around the city once and returned to the camp. So this they did six days. (15) But it came to pass on the seventh day that they rose early, about the dawning of the day, and marched around the city seven times in the same manner. On that day only they marched around the city seven times. (16) And the seventh time it happened, when the priests blew the trumpets that Joshua said to the people: 'Shout, for the Lord has given you the city! (17) Now the city shall be doomed by the Lord to destruction, it and all who are in it. Only Rahab the harlot shall live, she and all who are with her in the house, because she hid the messengers that we sent. (18) And you, by all means abstain from the accursed things, lest you become accursed when you take of the accursed things, and make the camp of Israel a curse, and trouble it. (19) But all the silver and gold and vessels of bronze and iron, are consecrated to the Lord; they shall come into the treasury of the Lord.' (20) So the people shouted when the priests blew the trumpets. And it happened when the people heard the sound of the*** *trumpet, and the people shouted with a great shout, that the wall fell down flat. Then the people went up into the city, every man straight before him, and they took the city."* Visualize that my friend, 40,000 men of war, mighty men of valor marching around the city every day for six days not uttering a single word. Can you hear the sound of trumpets blowing loudly with the Ark of the Covenant in the midst and the soldiers marching in step? I can imagine the sound of their footsteps being as the sound of thunder echoing off the wall of the city. Every day was an act of obedience and an act of faith. I certainly do not intend to oversimplify all of the dynamics that took place on this day of conquest, yet the people conquered their enemy and the walls of the city fell flat because of a shout. They split the ear of their adversary. How glorious is that day when the walls of fear and the walls of limitations that are attempting to box you in and keep you grounded are crushed like powder when you dare to offer up a shout unto the Lord. Imagine the untapped potential that's locked up inside of you that can be released when you get a *ruwa (roo-ah)* or a shout in your spirit. How many times have you wanted to scream when you were in the middle of a difficult situation? It's okay. Do it! However don't scream because of your present state of frustration, but rather shout because of your impending victory that lies ahead. Split the ear of your adversary and release your war cry. Sound the alarm from the holy mountain of God and declare to yourself that things are turning around for me. Your shout says that I may have been bound by some things and even by some people but now I'm being liberated. Look at the seemingly insurmountable mountain that may be standing in your way and get a Zerubbabel anointing. *"Who art thou, O great mountain? Before Zerubbabel! Thou shall become a plain! And he shall*

bring forth the headstone with shouts of Grace, grace unto it." (Zechariah 4:7). I pray my friend that you will not be afraid to affect your future by opening your mouth and declaring the great things that God desires to do in your life. Your shout is about more than making noise. It's about praising the Lord. Your shout is about praising your way through adversity and into to your place of victory.

Shout with a voice of triumph,
Shout with a voice of praise,
Shout with a voice of triumph,
Shout with a voice of praise,
Shout unto God for the victory,
Hey, Hey, Hey
Give the Lord a shout of praise!!

A WAR CRY PRAYER

Thank you heavenly Father, for allowing our victory to have a voice. May each reader gain a greater confidence in their praise and begin to forcefully declare his/her independence from the grips of sin and evil. Grant them the ability to not be afraid to lift up their voices like a trumpet and to release the war cry that dwells deep within every believer. May they find victory over adversity as they shout unto the Lord with a voice of triumph. This I sincerely pray for my friends.

In Jesus' name,

Amen.

CHAPTER 4

THE WEAPONS OF WARFARE

KNOWING IS HALF THE BATTLE

II Corinthians 10:3-4, *"(3) For though we walk in the flesh, we do not war according to the flesh. (4) For the weapons of our warfare are not carnal but mighty through God to the pulling down of strongholds.*

Ephesians 6:12, *"For we wrestle not against flesh and blood, but against principalities, against powers, against the rulers of the darkness of this age, against spiritual host of wickedness in the heavenly places."*

I began this chapter with those two scriptures to allow you to see the importance of knowing what type of battle you are in.

Knowing the environment and arsenal of your enemy is important so that you will know how to properly arm yourself in order to gain an advantage over and ultimately overcome your adversary. How much sense would it make as our country fights this current war on terrorism, if we were to send our soldiers into the war zone on horseback with a spear and shield while our opponent is armed with tanks, semiautomatic rifles and fighter jets? It would be obvious that we that we had not chosen the right weapons for the battle. The aforementioned passages state clearly that our battle is not a physical fleshly fight, it is spiritual. Though your problems or circumstances are played out in the realm of the earth, the spiritual connotations behind them are far greater than the eye can behold. This should help us to understand that our fight is not against our spouses, co-workers, co-laborers in ministry and other people that push us to the edge and make us almost lose it. Yet this is exactly what your enemy wants you to do and that is to lose it-- lose your faith, lose your witness, lose your hope, lose your sanity and most of all lose your fight. Have you ever seen anyone just give up on living? I'm not speaking of someone who was literally near physical death and now they have gone on to be with the Lord. I'm talking about a person that was once vibrant, sharp and upwardly mobile. A person that you said was going places and now because of a hard moment in their life they remain stuck in that moment. They really believe that their best days are behind them and that life has nothing more to offer them than their present reality or state of being. Having experienced a few disappointments and set-backs in life myself, I have learned that in hard times you either hold on through the storm and fight or you lie down and let your problems consume you. When you choose the latter course of action, before long life and even the ministry of the Lord slowly passes you by. It is my sincerest prayer that you develop the courage to fight your adversary to the fullest and then some. If you are presently experiencing some adversity in your life I encourage you as Paul instructed Timothy to **"endure hardness as a good soldier."** (II Timothy 2:3). This is by no means an attempt to belittle your hardship, but sometimes we need to be pushed to stop crying and to start praying. Stop doubting and start believing. Stop procrastinating and start doing. What Paul was actually telling Timothy is that in order to do this work you will need to be spiritually tough. The first thing that the Marine Corps develops in its new recruits is mental and physical toughness. No cowards need apply. Your trials or afflictions are nothing more than training maneuvers that are designed to develop a spiritual toughness in you so that when you are in the heat of a spiritual battle, you won't quit. Daniel 11:32b states **"but the people that know their God shall be strong and carry our great exploits."** We will have interesting or daring achievements, noble acts and heroic deeds. Knowing God will give you the ability to carry on with the plans that he has for your life even when things don't seem to be lining up with the plan. When you decide to go beyond a surface knowledge of the Lord and go on to know him by experience, you'll soon realize that the testing periods in your life is when you really solidify your relationship with the Father. So don't allow yourself to become discouraged or overly distressed if you find yourself in a tight predicament. Just know that your slight discomfort right now can't even be compared to the victory and triumph over life's circumstances that God will allow you to experience if you take a stand and contend for the faith. **"Therefore, gird up the loins of your mind, be sober, and** *rest your hope fully upon the grace that is to be brought to you at the revelation of Jesus Christ."* (I Peter 1:13)

THE SECRET WEAPON

When the average believer hears the term spiritual warfare, our minds automatically shift to the *"whole armor of God"* in Ephesians 6:11 and that is not necessarily a bad thing. We need our loins girded with truth and our hearts protected by the breastplate of righteousness and all the other remaining pieces of the armor. They are very important indeed. Though when they are observed closely you'll soon discover that these pieces of equipment are not weapons *(except the sword of the Spirit)*, but rather they are protective parts or coverings. They enable us to take a defensive stance when we are opposed by the devil. However no army goes to war with only armor to deflect their enemy's firepower, but they show up for battle with a full cache of weapons so that they might launch their own offensive attack against the adversary. Hence our secret weapon comes into play. It is not really a secret, for Jesus often talked about it and openly shows us through example. It seems like a secret to most of us because we so seldom use it. Yet this is a powerful force that is able to destroy strongholds, break generational curses, and undo heavy burdens. That secret weapon my friend is prayer and fasting. Mark 9:28-29, *"(28) And when He had come into the house, His disciples asked Him privately, 'Why could we not cast him out?' (29) So He said to them, 'This kind can come out by nothing but prayer and fasting.'"* If you back up a few verses starting at 17, you'll see the account of the father who had brought his son to Jesus which had a mute spirit after first presenting him to the disciples but they could not cast out the demon. Many of us have been trying to rid ourselves of some demons or of some negative recurring cycles in our lives and it seems as if we can't break free of these things. These kind come out by nothing but prayer and fasting. Fasting shows the Lord that you are serious about changing your conditions and that you are willing to deny yourself, turn down your plate and seek his guidance concerning your turnaround. It is showing God that we are taking our hands completely off of this thing except to fully engage ourselves to fasting and prayer. Notice the word engage. It means to participate or to commit yourself to something. In other words, if you are fasting then you must definitely couple it together with prayer, and if you are praying, somewhere in the midst of all your praying, there must also be some fasting. A few years ago our church completed the first of many 21 day fasting and prayer summits and in all my days of serving the Lord, I had never experienced such a powerful move of God. Each weekday the church was open at 6am, 12 noon and 6pm for one hour of prayer. On Saturday the church was open at 6am and 12 noon and Sunday mornings at 7:30am. It did not matter what hour or what day you chose to come and pray; the Lord was present to meet you. I thank God for this time of fasting. It allowed me to get a new perspective on serving God. Some strongholds and limitations that I had placed on myself were broken. A spirit of intimidation that was plaguing my life was crushed like powder. Philippians 4:13 became very real to me, *"I can do all things through Christ that strengthens me."* That time of fasting allowed me to hear God clearly and to share my thoughts of obtaining victory in spite of adversity on the pages of the book you now hold. Fasting and prayer gives you supernatural strength and the courage to do things that are beyond your scope of ability. Matthew 4:1-11, *"(1) Then Jesus was led up by the Spirit into the wilderness to be tempted by the devil. (2) And when he had fasted forty days and forty nights, afterward He was hungry. (3) Now when the tempter came to Him, he said, 'If You are the Son of God, command these stones become bread.' (4) But He answered and said, 'It is written, Man shall not live by bread alone, but by every word that proceeds from the mouth of God.' (5) Then the devil took Him up into the holy city, set Him on the pinnacle of the temple, (6) and said to Him, 'If You are the Son of God, throw Yourself down. For it is written: He shall give His angels charge over you, and In their hands they shall bear you up, Lest you dash your foot against a stone.' (7) Jesus said to him, 'It is written again, You shall not tempt the Lord thy God.' (8) Again, the devil took Him up on an exceedingly high mountain, and showed Him all the kingdoms of the world and their glory. (9) And he said to Him, 'All these things I will give You if You will fall down and worship me.' (10) Then Jesus said to him, 'Away with you, Satan! For it is written, You shall worship the Lord your God, and Him only you shall serve.' (11) Then the devil left Him, and behold, angels came and ministered to Him."* What a great testimony of strength and a powerful example of not allowing your flesh to rule over you. Prayer and fasting puts the Spirit in the driver's seat so that we won't make decisions in our flesh that will cause us to wreck our destiny. The important thing is to align yourself with God so that you can be sensitive to the Spirit and you can hear him prompting you to fast. *"Is this not the fast that I have chosen: To loose the bonds of wickedness, To undo heavy burdens, To let the oppressed go free, And that you break every yoke?"* (Isaiah 58:6).

Saints of God, let us be careful that we don't abandon the practice of fasting. In today's culture with so many vices pulling on us on a daily basis, there is not a shortage of things that we can fast from. However, we don't want to get to the point where we start to think of fasting as merely the act of giving up something. Fasting is actually abstaining from food for a spiritual purpose. Along with that fasting or sacrificing, we must also be bombarding the heavenlies with many prayers and supplication. If you really want to put the devil to flight and gain great victories in areas of your life that you have struggled with continually, put some prayer and fasting on it. Take some time and observe the scriptures and you'll discover that many times when the people of God were faced with great opposition, they turned their hearts to prayer and fasting and the Lord delivered them in a great way. There are great benefits my friend in prayer and fasting. **"(8) Then your light shall break forth in the morning, Your healing shall spring forth speedily, And your righteousness shall go before you; The glory of the Lord shall be your rear guard. (9) Then you shall call, and the Lord will answer; You shall cry, and He will say, Here am I."** (Isaiah 58:8-9). Prayerfully by now we know and believe that the Lord is with us and that He will lead us on into victory. There is no cause to retreat or turn back because we can be assured that as we go forth in our prayer and fasting that the Lord is going before us and all things are working together for our good.

A WARFARE PRAYER

Father I praise you for protecting us during our times of adversity and spiritual warfare. Help us to understand that our fight is not against the things or the people that we see, but it is against those things that we do not see. Strengthen each reader that they do not lose their mind, lose their faith, or lose their fight as they travel through their valley experiences. Help us to engage our adversary with every spiritual weapon that you have provided for us. Grant us the wisdom to know that some of our victories will not be obtained except that we turn to fasting and prayer. Bless each reader Lord, exceedingly and abundantly above all that they can ask or think.

In Jesus' name,

Amen.

CHAPTER 5

NO RETREAT

Now that we know and understand our weapons of warfare, we can now fully engage our adversary and steadily advance the Kingdom of God. When you are in pursuit of peace, success, victory, healing, prosperity and deliverance, you must be relentless in your efforts and retreating is not an option. To retreat means to withdraw, especially when under attack. For far too long the average believer has retreated at the first sign of opposition. We have a tendency to lie down and let Satan steamroll right over us. Judges 6:2-4 shows us a retreat in full effect. *"(2) And the hand of Midian prevailed against Israel. Because of the Midianites, the children of Israel made for themselves the dens, the caves, and the strongholds which are in the mountains. (3) So it was, whenever Israel had sown, Midianites would come up; also Amalekites and the people of the East would come up against them. (4) Then they would encamp against them and destroy produce of the earth as far as Gaza, and leave no sustenance for Israel, neither sheep nor ox nor donkey."* The children of Israel would retreat and hide in the caves of the mountains as their antagonist would invade their city and steal all of the harvest that they had worked so hard in sowing and growing. But thanks be unto God for raising up Gideon and calling him to be a mighty man of valor. By his hand was the Midianites destroyed with just 300 men. By Gideon's obedience to the word of the Lord, the retreating had stopped and they took the fight to the Midianites. *"(19) So Gideon and the hundred men who were with him came to the outpost of the camp at the beginning of the middle watch, just as they had posted the watch; and they blew the trumpets and broke the pitchers that were in their hands. (20) Then the three companies blew the trumpets and broke the pitchers— they held the torches in their left hands and the trumpets in their right hands for blowing—and they cried, 'The sword of the Lord and of Gideon!' (21) And every man stood in his place all around the camp; and the whole army ran and cried out and fled. (22) When the three hundred blew the trumpets, the Lord set every man's sword against his companion throughout the whole camp; and the army fled to Beth Acacia, toward Zererah, as far as the border of Abel Meholah, by Tabbath."* (Judges 7:19-22) I enjoy watching the gladiators in movies such as Troy, 300 and Alexander. The battle scenes get my adrenaline flowing as I see two great armies approaching the war zone from opposite ends of the terrain. Each troop encompassing the land with a massive and impressive display of courage and might; both armies full of confidence with no contemplation of turning back. Oh the day that we can have that same kind of confidence of anticipating a great victory over whatever trials we may face.

REMEMBER THE PAST VICTORIES

Many times the motivation you need in order to overcome your present set of adverse circumstances is to remember the times that God has delivered you in the past. This takes the pressure off of you and shows God that you trust him to deliver you just as he did in times past. Yet in the midst of our fiery trials, we seem to forget the countless times that the Lord has taken something that was meant for evil or to harm us and turned it around for our good. (Genesis 50:20). When we begin to realize how great our God is even as we are faced with unfavorable conditions, our response will then be, this too shall pass. Let's take a brief moment and look at young David when he was sent to the battlefield to take his brothers some food. I Samuel 17:31-37, *"(31) Now when the words which David spoke were heard, they reported them to Saul; and he sent for him. (32) Then David said to Saul, 'Let no man's heart fail because of him; your servant will go and fight with this Philistine.' (33) And Saul said to David, 'You are not able to go against this Philistine to fight with him; for you are a youth and he a man of war from his youth.' (34) But David said to Saul, 'Your servant used to keep his father's sheep and when a lion or a bear came and took a lamb out of the flock, (35) I went out after it and struck it, and delivered the lamb from its mouth; and when it arose against me, I caught it by its beard, and struck it and killed it. (36) Your servant has killed both lion and bear; and this uncircumcised Philistine shall be like one of them, seeing he has defied the armies of the living God.' (37) Moreover David said, "the Lord, who delivered me from the paw of the lion and from the paw of the bear, He will deliver me from the hand of this Philistine. And Saul said to David, 'Go, and the Lord be with you.'"* David was simply saying to King Saul, God's got this! I've fought and destroyed wild beast of the field, who is this mere mortal man that dares to defy God's people. This is the attitude that we should display as we continue to fight from our place of victory. It is essential that we remember what God has already done in our lives and discern that he is able to do even greater than his former mighty acts. *"Now to Him who is able to do exceedingly abundantly above all that we ask or think, according to the power that works in us."* (Ephesians 3:20). Think about it, after all that you have faced and gone through and yet you are still standing, still believing, and still praising. What is this light affliction that dares to stand in your way now? For *"many are the afflictions of the righteous, but the Lord delivers him out of them all."* (Psalm 34:19). God is with you my friend. The challenge now is to let him work in you and through you. What was it that gave the Hebrew boys such great assurance in the power of God as they faced the probability of being executed in a flesh burning, bone dissolving pit of fire? Could it have been that they remembered that the Lord had already shown his saving ability to them once before? They were only taking a stand for God just as they had done previously when they had refused to partake of the king's delicacies and now they were determined not to be moved by the king's decree of idolatrous worship of a golden image. Daniel 1:11-15 *"(1) So Daniel said to the steward whom the chief of the eunuchs had set over Daniel, Hananiah, Mishael, And Azariah, (12) 'Please test your servants for ten days, and let them give us vegetables to eat and water to drink. (13) Then let our appearance be examined before you, and the appearance of the young men who eat the portion of the kings delicacies; and as you see fit, so deal with your servants.' (14) So he consented with them in this matter, and tested them ten days. (15) At the end of ten days their features appeared better and fatter in flesh than all the young men who ate the portion of the king's delicacies."* Now what, O King? We didn't eat your food and we are not going to worship your golden image. We are so confident in our God because he has already shown us that he is with us. We didn't eat the finest meats from the king's table yet we look better than those who consumed all that the king had to offer. Now you want us to bow down and worship an idol god? That is definitely out of the question. Daniel 3:17-18, *"(17) If that is the case, our God whom we serve is able to deliver us from the burning fiery furnace, and He will deliver us from your hand, O king. (18) but if not, let it be known to you, O king that we do not serve your gods, nor will we worship the gold image which you set up."* You can make it through whatever you are facing right now by remembering that the Lord is a mighty deliverer. Don't allow your storm or your worries to tower over you and taunt you as Goliath did the army of Israel. Place your confidence firmly in the Lord your God and relentlessly pursue your victory. Fight with all that's within you and then some. Don't let up lest you become fainthearted or small in your faith. Fight for your victory. Fight for your breakthrough. Fight for your deliverance. Fight for your harvest. Fight for your spiritual liberation. The day of victory is at hand. Success is now! Faith is now! Victory is now! Go, and the Lord be with you.

GOD IS WITH YOU

One of the greatest advantages of being a blood-washed, born-again believer is having the assurance that God is with you. From your Zion celebrations on the mountain to your Lodebar and wilderness experiences in the valley, God is with you. It is a good thing to know that the Lord is fighting for us and not against us. Nonetheless for a lot of us, when we go through our seasons of testing we soon forget that God is right there with us. *"If God be for us, who can be against us?"* (Romans 8:36b) King Jehoshaphat must have understood this when the Moabites, Ammonites and Edomites came to make war against Judah. Yes, fear did come upon him according to the scriptures for a great multitude was coming up against him; nevertheless the king turned his face and faith to God. He put God in remembrance of his word. Let's see how God responded. II Chronicles 20:14-17, *"(14) Then the Spirit of the Lord came upon Jahaziel the son of Zechariah, the son of Benaiah, the son Jeiel, the son of Mattaniah, a Levite of the sons of Asaph, in the midst of the assembly. (15) And he said, 'Listen, all you of Judah and you inhabitants of Jerusalem, and you, King Jehoshaphat! Thus says the Lord to you: Do not be afraid nor dismayed because of this great multitude, for the battle is not yours, but God's. (16) Tomorrow go down against them. They will surely come up by the Ascent of Ziz, and you will find them at the end of the brook before the Wilderness of Jeruel. (17) You will not need to fight in this battle. Position yourselves, stand still and see the salvation of the Lord, who is with you, O Judah and Jerusalem! Do not fear or dismayed; tomorrow go out against them, for the Lord is with you.'"* Hallelujah!! Is this not enough encouragement for you to stand in the face of your opposition without retreating knowing that the Lord is with you? Who can stand against you when God is with you? Even when the fight is clearly not in your favor, when you are in God you will win. You will succeed. My pastor has taught us for about the past few years that when God is with you, things great go for you. When you can't figure out how this thing is going to work or you think that you are about to go under, you are the perfect candidate for God to prove to you that he is with you. II Kings 6:8-17, *"(8) Now the King of Syria was making war against Israel; and he consulted with his servants, saying, my camp will be in such and such a place. (9) And the Man of God sent to the King of Israel, saying, 'Beware that you do not pass this place, for the Syrians are coming down there.' (10) Then the king of Israel sent someone to the place of which the Man of God had told him. Thus he warned him, and he was watchful there, not just once or twice. (11) Therefore the heart of the king of Syria was greatly troubled by this thing; and he called his servants and said to them, 'Will you not show me which of us is for the king of Israel?' (12) One of his servants said, 'None my lord, O king, but Elisha, the prophet who is in Israel, tells the king of the words that you speak in your bedroom.' (13) So he said, 'Go and see where he is, that I may send and get him.' And it was told him saying, 'Surely he is in Dothan.' (14) Therefore he sent horses and chariots and a great army there, and they came by night and surrounded the city. (15) And when the servant of the man of God arose early and went out, there was an army, surrounding the city with horses and chariots. And his servant said to him, 'Alas my master! What shall we do?' (16) So he answered, 'Do not fear, for those who are with us are more than those who are with them.' (17) And Elisha prayed, and said, 'Lord, I pray, open his eyes that he may see.' Then the Lord opened the eyes of the young man, and he saw. And behold, the mountain was full of horses and chariots of fire, all around Elisha."* What a powerful way for the Lord to show us that no matter what it is that we are facing, he is with us. God is with you my brother. Don't give up and abandon the ship that he has given you to guide. The Lord is with you my sister. Don't lose your sanity by worrying about how things are going to come together, for the prince of peace is with you. When your circumstances begin to press in on you, our God is in the realm of the unseen working on your behalf. That's why as we continue in our pursuit of victory, we cannot allow ourselves to be overwhelmed or overly concerned with what we see physically. Everything that we can literally see is temporal and subject to change at any moment in time. (II Corinthians 4:18) My friend situations and circumstances do change. Walls do come down. Giants…..they do die. The old adage declares that the bigger they are, the harder they fall. *"For when the enemy does come in like a flood, the Spirit of the Lord will lift up a standard against him."* (Isaiah 59:19). This reassures us that no matter what we are facing or how strenuous the trials may become, God is with us and your victory is not afar off. Endure this present hardness as a good soldier. Walk by faith. Trust the Lord to lead you in every situation and know that you are victorious through Jesus Christ.

A PRAYER FOR VICTORY

Blessed Father,

Thank you giving us the strength and power needed in order to endure and overcome our adversity. I pray for each fellow reader, that they won't retreat, but continue to move forward knowing that you are with each and every one of us. Help them to remember their past victories and to know that if you delivered them then, you can and will deliver them now. Thank you in advance for adjusting our attitudes that we won't live a life of defeat, but that we live everyday knowing that we have victory in Jesus Christ.

In Jesus' name I pray,

Amen.

www.ingramcontent.com/pod-product-compliance
Lightning Source LLC
Chambersburg PA
CBHW072037060426
42449CB00010BA/2309